100

THINGS TO DO IN
SPRINGFIELD, IL
BEFORE YOU
DIE

100

THINGS TO DO IN
SPRINGFIELD, IL
BEFORE YOU
DIE

● ●

PENNY ZIMMERMAN-WILLS

REEDY PRESS

Library of Congress Control Number: 2016937274

ISBN: 9781681060453

Design by Jill Halpin

Printed in the United States of America
16 17 18 19 20   5 4 3 2 1

Please note that websites, phone numbers, addresses, and company names are subject to change or cancellation. We did our best to relay the most accurate information available, but due to circumstances beyond our control, please do not hold us liable for misinformation. When exploring new destinations, please do your homework before you go.

DEDICATION

To my mom, Marlene, who always let me color outside the lines.

• •

CONTENTS

Music and Entertainment

● ●

Sports and Recreation

• •

Culture and History

• •

Land of Lincoln

Shopping and Fashion

• •

• •

PREFACE

Welcome to Springfield!

The capital city. Springpatch. Lincoln's hometown. However you look at it, Springfield is a wonderful city of rich history, beautiful Illinois prairie, delicious food (hello, horseshoes!), wineries, art galleries, and much more. My hope is that this book will help you have an adventure, discover something new, learn about history, and check things off your bucket list!

For visitors: This is meant to give you some great ideas on how to enjoy our city to the fullest, from well-known highlights like Lincoln's Home to hidden gems where you can find the best fried catfish or enjoy a scenic bike ride. This is only the beginning of what the city offers.

For locals: This is meant to inspire you to rediscover the great city you live in. When was the last time you visited Lincoln's Tomb and rubbed his bronze nose for luck? Have you enjoyed New Salem's Candlelight Tour or watched local theater under the stars at the Muni?

There are many more things to do than what is in this book—it was hard to narrow it down to just one hundred things. Surprised? You shouldn't be. There is a plethora of fun, unique, interesting ways to explore Springfield. So as you mark things off the list, I hope it leads to new discoveries.

• •

Writing this book has been a pleasure, from the wonderful people I've met to the sites I've discovered or rediscovered. Even though the title sounds a bit foreboding, don't worry. I'm sure you have plenty of time to search out all 100 things. Let's start now!

—Penny

Photo credit: Penny Zimmerman-Wills

FOOD AND DRINK

CRUNCH ON A KORNDOG
AT THE ILLINOIS STATE FAIR

Cozy dogs, pronto pups, corn dogs—no matter what you call them, there's no denying that hot dogs coated in cornmeal, deep fried and served on a stick are a staple of state fairs. But locals know nothing compares to a Vose's Korndog at the Illinois State Fair. The plump hot dogs are hand-dipped in a slightly sweet batter, fried in vegetable oil and placed upright in a basket for 2 ½ minutes to keep them crispy. Add a few stripes of mustard and munch on yours at Vose's stand, a family-owned fixture at the fairgrounds for four decades, as you take in the sights and sounds of Grandstand Avenue.

217-725-6701,
www.voseconcessions.com

CELEBRATE FARM FRESH
AT AMERICAN HARVEST EATERY

The chefs of American Harvest take pride in supporting local family farms and pesticide-free products. Menus are guided by the seasons, and comfort food is served with a twist. Even if you're not the type to nix French fries for vegetables, you'll change your mind after tasting the roasted Brussel sprouts prepared with dates, roasted peanuts, and cider gastrique. Dinner options such as ravioli with braised lamb or salmon with chickpea tomato stew pair well with an extensive craft beer and wine selection.

3241 W. Iles St., 217-546-8300,
www.americanharvesteatery.com

TIP
Visit this restaurant's older sibling, Augie's Front Burner, on Thrifty Thursdays for a locally sourced, three-course meal for $14.99.

109 S. Fifth St., 217-544-6979,
www.augiesfrontburner.com

PERUSE PRODUCE
AT THE FARMERS' MARKET

Saturday mornings at the Old State Capitol Farmers' Market are a shopping experience for the senses. The air is filled with the smells of freshly baked bread, bouquets of garden flowers, and herbs. Tables overflow with beautiful mounds of ruby red radishes, purple eggplant, and beans in every shade of green, making buying groceries at this open-air market fun. You can stock up on fresh produce, organic meat, eggs, plants, and cheese while you chat with the local vendors who grow them. After shopping, enjoy a breakfast taco (made with local chorizo, hand cut fries, and scrambled eggs) from StrEATside Bistro food truck while you stroll and enjoy some great dog (and people) watching. The market also operates Wednesday afternoons from May through October.

Adams Street between Fifth and Second streets, 217-544-1723, www.downtownspringfield.org,

StrEATside Bistro, 217-415-3852, www.cooperstreatside.com

TIP

An evening version, the Illinois Products Farmers' Market, is held on Thursday nights from May through October at The Shed at the state fairgrounds, with local food vendors, music, health-related activities, wine and beer. Event is free and open to the public.
801 Sangamon Ave., 217-785-4873,
www.illinoisproductmarket.com

PIG OUT ON POT PIE
AT CAFÉ MOXO

On a cold, wintry day, nothing warms you up like a homemade pot pie from this downtown café. Sure, you can't go wrong with breakfast options like cheddar biscuits and gravy or lunch staples like Fall Over (sausage, sweet potato, and pear) soup and Piggly Wiggly pulled pork sandwiches, but this is the dish that takes you back to Grandma's kitchen. This thick, savory blend of chicken and vegetables in a creamy roux topped with an egg-washed golden pie crust is the ultimate in comfort food. A family-size pie can be purchased to take and bake at home.

411 E. Adams St., 217-788-8084,
cafemoxo.com

HAVE BRUNCH
IN THE BEER GARDEN
AT BOONE'S SALOON

The beer garden at this corner bar is usually filled with legislative types and state workers during the week due to its proximity to the state capitol. But on weekends, it's the perfect place to nosh on blueberry bacon pancakes. The crowd is young and eclectic; the Bloody Mary is just spicy enough to cure what ails you, and most brunch dishes come with tater tots. Enough said.

301 W. Edwards St., 217-679-3752,
boonessaloon.com

Since this is central Illinois, there are no ocean or mountain views to celebrate, but here are a few more places to enjoy al fresco dining.

Papa Frank's
4111 Wabash Ave., 217-679-8700,
www.papafranksspringfield.com

The Corner Pub and Grill
3271 W. Iles Ave., 217-546-3600,
www.thecornerpubandgrill.com

Cooper's Hawk Winery & Restaurants
2501 Wabash Ave., 217-321-9100,
www.coopershawkwinery.com

Maldaner's
222 S. Sixth St., 217-522-4313,
www.maldaners.com

Obed and Isaac's Microbrewery and Eatery
500 S. Sixth St., 217-670-0627,
www.connshospitalitygroup.com

FEAST ON FRIED CHICKEN
AT THE TRACK SHACK

It's almost a secret that this no-frills bar by the railroad tracks serves the best fried chicken in town every Thursday night. Even in the Track Shack itself, the only evidence is a sign on the wall behind the counter. But folks in the know keep coming back for chicken that's fresh and crispy outside and piping hot and moist on the inside, due to being dipped in ice water before it's dredged in flour and spices. It comes with a couple sides and choice of potato, and one meal is enough for two to share. This chicken dinner is a winner winner.

233 E. Laurel St., 217-522-0444

PICK BLUEBERRIES
AT JEFFERIES ORCHARD

Sure, you can pick up a flat of fresh fruit at the local market, but it's more fun to take a drive to the country and pick your own blueberries, strawberries, and cherries. Starting around July 4th, there are four acres of blueberry bushes, all lined up in rows and loaded with ripe fruit, that require no bending or ladders, just your willpower to drop them in a bucket instead of your mouth. The picking season is short, usually lasting only about 10 days, so mark your calendars! Located just five miles north of the city, the stand is open daily from spring through fall.

1016 Jefferies Rd., 217-487-7582,
www.jefferies-orchard.com

TIP
Call ahead for picking schedules, which depend
on weather and fruit production.

INDULGE IN MACARONS
AT INCREDIBLY DELICIOUS

When you want to feel more *ooh-la-la* than *Land of Lincoln*, there's only one thing to do. Order a sampling of the daily flavors of French *macarons* like rose and pistachio and take a seat on the back porch of Incredibly Delicious. Enjoy the manicured courtyard garden surrounded by an antique iron fence and be transported to another place. While you're at it, you should sample the soup, salad, or quiche special as well. Just leave room for the pretty pastel meringue puffs made daily at this artisan bakery.

925 S. Seventh St., 217-528-8548,
www.incrediblydelicious.com

SAVOR SOUP
AT THE FEED STORE

For nearly three decades, this downtown spot has been ladling up delicious homemade soups to lunchtime crowds—up to 275 quarts a day of mushroom or tomato bisque, Wisconsin cheese, minestrone, French potato, and more. Summer soups include gazpacho and strawberry. They keep it simple—soup, sandwiches, and desserts—but the formula works. There's even a "no choice" option for those who can't make a decision, which is a sandwich, cup of soup, and beverage for under $9. Take a window seat in this hectic yet cozy Lincoln-era brick building for a clear view of the Old State Capitol. You never know who you might see—President Obama likes to stop by when he's in town for the beef barley soup and a turkey sandwich.

516 E. Adams St., 217-528-3355

TRY THE HEAT
AT MAGIC KITCHEN

Magic Kitchen is like no other Thai restaurant. First of all, it's housed in a former gas station, redecorated with knotty pine paneling. Second, on warm summer nights, people bring coolers full of wine and beer (no liquor license) and hang out in the parking lot to wait for a table. Finally, the desserts are almost mandatory for many customers, who refer to the restaurant as "Thai and pie." The food is great, whether it's the crispy egg rolls with peanut sauce, pad thai, or red curry with coconut milk. You can order the level of heat you want in your dish, but if you get too cocky and order anything above mild plus, prepare to sweat.

4112 N. Peoria Rd., 217-525-2230,
www.magickitchenthai.com

TIP

Bring cash and a cooler. The restaurant serves no
alcohol and does not accept credit cards.
A second location can be found at
115 N. Lewis St., 217-525-6975.

TAKE A TOUR
OF ROLLING MEADOWS BREWERY

Find out where the popular Lincoln's Lager and Abe's Ale come from. For a $10 fee, you can tour this rural craft brewery, sample its brews, and take home a tasting glass. Using only local ingredients and fresh water from its onsite well to produce its Springfield Wheat and other brews, the facility also makes great dog treats. Call ahead to schedule a tour.

3954 Central Point Rd., Cantrall, 217-899-7239,
www.rmbrewery.com

The local craft beer scene is alive and well.
Here are a few more you should try:

Obed and Isaac's Microbrewery and Eatery
500 S. Sixth St., 217-670-0627,
www.connshospitalitygroup.com

Engrained Brewing Co.
1120 W. Lincolnshire Blvd, Springfield,
217-546-3054,
www.engrainedbrewing.com

Spirited Republic
509 Pulaski St., Lincoln, 217-605-0475,
www.spiritedrepublic.com

STAND IN LINE
FOR CATFISH
AT CARTER'S FISH MARKET

Ever stand in line in a snow storm to eat fried fish? Yeah, people do that here for fried walleye, catfish, and scored buffalo fish. Of course, there's usually a line in all kinds of weather at this tiny wooden shack with the take-out window, attached to a fresh fish market. Just take a number and hang out for a few—it's worth it! One fish platter includes pickles and onions, and is enough to share.

1900 S. Grand Ave. E., 217-525-2571,
www.cartersfishmarkets.com

DIG IN TO A HORSESHOE
AT D'ARCY'S PINT

Here's the deal: Every place in town has a version of a horseshoe—a local signature dish made with a layer of meat (from Buffalo chicken to breaded tenderloin) over toast, topped with French fries and slathered in…wait for it…thick, creamy cheese sauce. It's gluttonous goodness. But D'Arcy's is the best. And everyone knows it, so it's always crowded and you'll have to wait for a table.

661 W. Stanford Ave., 217-494-8800,
www.darcyspintonline.com

TASTE WINE
AT DANENBERGER FAMILY VINEYARDS

This upscale winery is more for the sophisticated sippers than the drink-anything-you-put-in-front-of-me's. Nestled in the countryside among cornfields, this lush vineyard is a relaxing place to enjoy a velvety glass (or two) of wine before a game of bocce ball. The charming Tasting Room is the perfect setting to sample red, white, or rosé, from a splash to a one-ounce pour. Or enjoy a picnic on the terrace, as the owners' friendly huskies stroll the grounds and greet customers. Visit on Thursday or Friday for more personal assistance from the winemaker. Wood-fired pizzas and a limited menu of gourmet bites like filet sliders and corn chowder prepared by a local chef are offered on Sundays.

12341 Irish Road, New Berlin, 217-488-6321,
www.danenbergerfamilyvineyards.com

The Illinois wine industry is fast growing.
Here are a few more local wineries to check out:

Hill Prairie Winery
23753 Lounsberry Rd., Oakford, 217-635-9900,
www.hillprairiewinery.com

West of Wise
14096 IL/Route 97, Petersburg, 217-632-6003,
www.westofwise.com

Walnut Street Winery
309 S. Walnut St., Rochester, 217-498-9800,
www.walnutstreetwinery.com

SAVOR CHILLI
AT THE DEW CHILLI PARLOR

Sit at the counter and order the Dew Double Header, a tamale dunked in a bowl of chilli, and you'll see why this is a legend in the world of Springfield chilli. (Yes, it's sometimes spelled with two L's here. A state resolution even proclaims Springfield the Chilli Capital of the Civilized World.) The tiny tan brick building holds about 10 tables, and its floor is covered in 120,000 pennies. The owner keeps the secret spice blend recipe in half, in two separate local bank vaults. We told you: they take their chilli serious here.

121 S. Fifth St., 217-679-1910,
www.dewchilliparlor.com

TIPS
On-street parking is scarce,
but customers can park in the McDonald's lot next door.

One "L" or two, Springfield chil[l]i is worth sampling.
Here are some other places to get a fix of America's favorite spicy stew:

Cook's Spice Rack
910 N. Grand Ave W., 217-492-2695,
www.cookspicerack.com

The Chili Parlor (one "L")
820 S. Ninth St., 217-523-4989,
www.thechiliparloronline.com

SAMPLE SEASONAL MOREL PIE
AT MALDANER'S

In operation since 1884, the oldest restaurant in town is a blend of rich history and farm-to-table philosophy. A rooftop garden provides some of the restaurant's vegetables and herbs for traditional favorites like beef Wellington and rack of lamb, and rooftop hives provide honey for desserts. But one delicacy is only available each spring, if Mother Nature cooperates: morel pie, a blend of morel mushrooms, butter, spring onions, cream, herbs, and cheese baked in a pie crust. Slide into a green leather seat in the corner of the regal bar area and people watch while you indulge in this seasonal concoction.

222 S. Sixth St., 217-522-4313,
www.maldaners.com

CULTIVATE YOUR SKILLS
IN CAROL JEAN'S COOKING CLASS

Maybe butternut squash flan isn't your cup of tea, but it could be with a little help from some new friends and the culinary team of Carol Jean Fraase and Sara Workman. Bring your own apron and spend three hours preparing and cooking a gourmet meal in Fraase's cottage in the country. The event is equal parts social hour, instruction, and feeding frenzy with just one rule: wine is only served once ingredients are chopped. Classes are held three nights a week in February and March. And you don't have to do dishes.

782 S. Farmingdale Rd., New Berlin, 217-546-3091,
www.caroljeancuisine.com

Other good sources to hone your cooking skills:

Lincoln Land Community College Culinary Institute
5250 Shepherd Rd., 217-786-2292,
www.llcc.edu/community-education/culinary-institute

Copper Pot Cooking Studio
916 W. Laurel St., 217-220-3870,
www.copperpotclasses.com

BLOW YOUR DIET FOR CHOCOLATE
AT COCOA BLUE

Peanut clusters, dark chocolate candied orange peel, passion fruit truffles, sea salt caramels. Do we have your attention yet? Lawyer turned chocolatier Joshua Becker's love for chocolate, which began as a teenager living in the Netherlands, is evident in his tiny shop tucked inside a restored Town Hall building. Perfect, shiny chocolate in all forms—covering peanuts, coating apples, and swirled over peanut butter—is sourced from around the world, from Belgium and France to Switzerland. Truffles in flavors like coconut, key lime, hazelnut brandy, mint, raspberry, and champagne sit on glass shelves next to clusters of white, milk, and dark coated cashews and chunks of dark chocolate chili pepper bark. Ice cream, coffee, and hot chocolate concoctions are also served. A second location can be found at 4015 Yucan Dr., Springfield.

117 E. Main St., Rochester, 217-498-1261,
www.cocoabluechocolates.com

EAT A PLATE-SIZED PANCAKE
AT CHARLIE PARKER'S DINER

This kitschy, 50s-style diner and former bait shop serves up huge portions in a World War II-era Quonset hut. Yes, it offers meatloaf, cheeseburgers, omelets, and all the rest, but it's the 10-inch, plate-sized pancakes that are the real highlight. And if you're *really* hungry, try the even bigger, pizza-sized versions. Finish four of them and you get a free meal and the thrill of victory. But that's probably not going to happen.

700 North St., 217-241-2104,
www.charlieparkersdiner.net

SIP A CUP
OF JAVA ON THE PORCH
AT WM. VAN'S COFFEE HOUSE

You can enjoy a cup of custom-roasted Abe's Blend inside the cozy, brick, Lincoln Era home, decorated with barn wood, old theater lighting, and vintage photos. But the best place to enjoy a cup is on one of the pet-friendly outdoor porches.

503 S. Seventh St., 217-679-4726,
www.connshospitalitygroup.com

Springfield has a number of locally-owned gourmet coffee shops. Here are a few to choose from:

Custom Cup
Stop by this small shop to order a bag of small-batch, fresh-roasted, single-origin, direct-trade coffee. You can choose the roast level, and the owners will gladly give you tips on how best to brew your coffee at home. Then grab a cup to go, but do so early, because it's only open till 1 p.m.
321 E. Monroe St., 217-652-7279,
www.customcupofcoffee.com

Grab-A-Java
Not only does the city's first gourmet coffee drive-through provide a good cup of joe-to-go, but the owner's artwork on the large sign out front—usually depicting on-point topical satire—adds a good dose of humor to your visit. And if you ask, they'll give you coffee grounds for your garden.
1702 S. Sixth St., 217-523-5282;
3115 Hedley Road, 217-698-9773

Andiamo
Nestled downtown near the Old State Capitol, the friendly crew here serves up a long list of espresso drinks and is a great place for a lunch break while you shop at the Old State Capitol Art Fair.
204 S. Sixth St., 217-523-3262, www.cafeandiamo.com

The Bean Counter
Stop by for Red Eye (coffee and espresso mix) and a cinnamon roll, and take home a bag of Monster or Morningssuk Blend beans. Don't leave without checking out the owner's other business next door, Bombadil Studios, for antiques and jewelry.
1911 W. Isles, 217-546-4740,
www.encounterthecounter.com

DRIVE-THROUGH
THE MAID-RITE

This is the easiest food order you'll ever make. The only entree is the Maid-Rite sandwich, a moist—but not greasy—blend of loose ground beef, onion, mustard, savory spices, and a hint of garlic. (Picture a sloppy joe without the sauce.) Your only decision is whether to get it with cheese or without. Well, technically, you also have to decide whether or not to get fries and what to drink, but that's easy—you want it with fries and the homemade root beer. This tiny white building, which claims to have had the country's first drive-thru window, isn't much to look at. But the sandwich that made it famous has been served up at this spot on the legendary Route 66 since 1924 and is well worth the trip.

118 N. Pasfield St., 217-523-0723,
www.maid-rite.com

ENJOY LIBATIONS WITH A VIEW
IN THE PINNACLE CLUB LOUNGE

Okay, so we admit that the Capital City is pretty flat. But that's not a bad thing when you're on the 30th floor of the Wyndham Springfield City Centre. You can have an unobstructed view of all the lights of the city twinkling below as you indulge in a chocolate martini while seated in the Pinnacle Club Lounge. Soak up more of the view with dinner at Nick and Nino's Steakhouse, located on the other side of the City Centre penthouse.

700 E. Adams St., 217-789-1530,
www.nickandninospringfield.com

PICK UP A DOZEN DONUTS
AT MEL-O-CREAM

Legend says that when this local company was founded in 1932, a secret formula base called "cream" was used to make the donuts. What the Mel-O portion of the name means is still up in the air. But locals can't get enough of these glazed, powdered, and cream-filled pastries. The company, which now mainly manufactures and supplies frozen dough products throughout the Midwest, still operates a few local retail bakeries. Grab a dozen and don't forget the milk. Other locations: 3010 S. 6th St., 217-529-7708; 1953 W. Monroe St., 217-546-4651; 525 E. North Grand Ave., 217-528-2303.

217 E. Laurel St., 217-544-4644,
www.mel-o-cream.com

GRAB A BAG TO GO
AT DEL'S

Shopping the eclectic shops on Sixth Street will make you hungry, so swing by Del's Popcorn Shop Inc. for a bag of freshly popped corn. While you're there, watch the fluffy white popcorn tossed with caramel or cheese in large copper kettles through the front windows. Try one of the mouth-watering specialty flavors like White Chocolate Caramel Corn or Del's Deluxe (caramel corn with almonds, pecans, and coconut). This old-fashioned confectionery also sells nuts, candy, and ice cream. A second location is at 3013 Lindbergh Blvd.

213 S. Sixth St., 217-544-0037,
www.delspopcornshop.com

MUSIC AND ENTERTAINMENT

SEE A SHOW
UNDER THE STARS
AT THE MUNI

Live theater is great. Combine it with warm summer breezes, a picnic basket, maybe the occasional bug, and you have a Springfield tradition. Since 1950, when a fifty-five acre wheat field was transformed into a not-for-profit theatrical amphitheater, the Springfield Municipal Opera Association has been delighting audiences and enticing local actors to volunteer their time and energy to entertain. The Muni, one of the largest community theaters in the Midwest, produces four shows each season at its lakeside setting. It has 815 reserved seats, but it's more fun to bring your lawn chairs or share a family picnic on a blanket on the grass.

815 E. Lake Shore Dr., 217-793-6864,
www.themuni.org

For a more intimate, historic twist on outdoor theater, watch a Theatre in the Park production at Lincoln's New Salem in Petersburg from mid-June to late August.

15588 History Ln., Petersburg, 217-632-5440, www.theatreinthepark.net

RIDE TO THE TOP OF THE FERRIS WHEEL
AT SCHEELS

Sure, you can shop the massive Scheels sporting goods store for a new pair of Nikes, fishing supplies, or fashion accessories, or get your skates sharpened in one of the service shops aimed at keeping you in an active lifestyle. But that 65-foot Ferris wheel in the center of the building just dares you to ride to the top. So do it, then watch the tropical fish in the sixteen thousand gallon saltwater aquarium.

3801 S. MacArthur Blvd., 217-726-6330,
www.scheels.com

SPEND A ROMANTIC WEEKEND
AT INN AT 835

You don't have to be an out-of-towner to enjoy this cozy inn. It's the perfect place to celebrate a special occasion with a loved one. What better way to rev up the romance in your life than spending the weekend in the spacious three-room Orchid Suite, with fireplace, king iron bed, and private veranda with a view of the State Capitol? Begin the day with gourmet coffee or tea and served-to-order breakfast, and enjoy the evening with a glass of wine in the sitting room. Boost the romance factor even more with an amenity package, like red roses in the room or champagne breakfast in bed. Each of the eleven guest rooms ooze with unique features, antiques, and charm. The inn, designed during the Arts and Crafts Movement by one of the area's leading architects, was once one of the city's premier homes because of its detailed oak woodwork, massive fireplaces and airy verandas. Today, the renovated Classical Revival—on the National Register of Historic Places—spoils guests with its stately charm. But don't worry; you'll still be able to enjoy modern conveniences like cable TV and Wi-Fi. Of course if you're enjoying a romantic weekend away from home, you shouldn't need them.

835 S. Second St., 217-523-4466,
www.connshospitalitygroup.com

HEAR BELLS
AT THE INTERNATIONAL CARILLON FESTIVAL

Each year, the festival celebrates the unique instrument that is a collection of bells played by a keyboard. With sixty-seven bells, Washington Park's Thomas Rees Memorial Carillon is one of the world's largest. The sounds that emanate from the 132-foot concrete, brick, and steel tower suggest a chime on steroids, and the festival is your one chance to hear it played by professionals from around the world. You can also take a tour to the top and attend free weekly concerts.

1740 W. Fayette Ave. and Chatham Road, 217-546-3853,
www.carillon-rees.org.

TIP
Don't miss one of the best free fireworks shows around on the final night of the festival.

GLIDE DOWN THE GIANT SLIDE
AT THE ILLINOIS STATE FAIR

Sure there are cute goats, antique tractors, 80s rock bands in the Grandstand and all the food on a stick you can inhale, but you haven't properly done the State Fair unless you've slid down the giant neon-yellow slide near the main gate. The kids spring up the hundred steps to the top, while their adult companions usually trek up a little slower. But everyone laughs on the way down.

Illinois State Fair, 801 E. Sangamon Ave., 217-782-1698,
www.agr.state.il.us

EXPLORE NEW SALEM
BY CANDLELIGHT

Exploring this 1830s village where Abraham Lincoln lived as a young man is always fun, but the popular fall Candlelight Tour puts a different spin on the New Salem State Historic Site. The cabins are lit only by candles and firelight. Lanterns light the paths between the twelve log homes, ten artisan workshops, schoolhouse, and tavern. Kids with red and green glow sticks add a surreal touch. You can watch volunteers demonstrate skills like spinning wool, enjoy a little bluegrass music, or simply soak up the atmosphere.

15588 History Lane, Petersburg, 217-632-4000,
www.lincolnsnewsalem.com

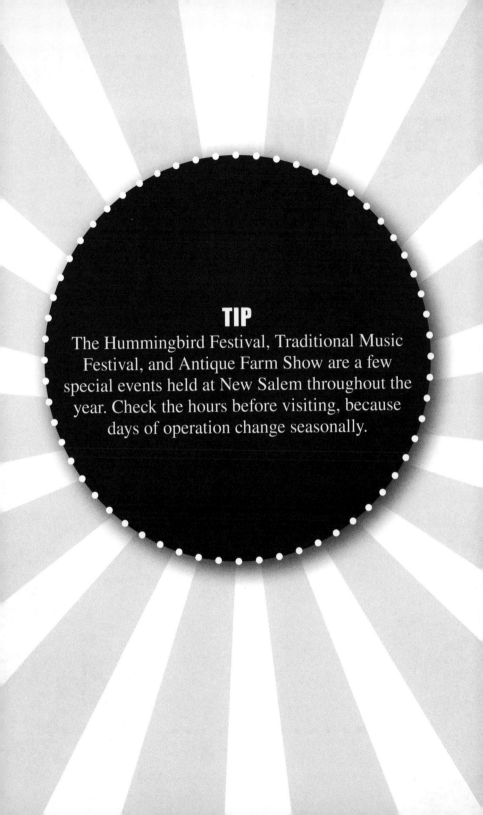

TIP

The Hummingbird Festival, Traditional Music Festival, and Antique Farm Show are a few special events held at New Salem throughout the year. Check the hours before visiting, because days of operation change seasonally.

ENJOY OPEN-AIR CINEMA
AT THE ROUTE 66 TWIN DRIVE-IN

Make the most of a warm summer night by watching cinema in the great outdoors. Route 66 Twin Drive-In features two screens, each showing double features that start at sundown. You can watch from the car while munching popcorn and enjoying the breeze, or bring lawn chairs and set up a little outdoor theater for the entire family. The drive-in is open on weekends from April through October, and seven nights a week in the summer. A great way to finish the evening, after spending the day next door at Knight's Action Park, an outdoor entertainment complex with pedal boats, water slides, mini-golf, and go-karts.

1700 Recreation Drive, 217-698-0066,
www.route66-drivein.com

JAM FOR CHARITY
AT SOHO MUSIC FESTIVAL

Two days, five states, 60 bands. This music jam benefits local charities. Every June, this family-friendly outdoor event fills the streets of downtown with the sound of live music, children's laughter, and lots of clapping. A list of local, regional, and national artists giving live performances of original music is the backbone of the festival, which also includes art and food vendors, a 10K race, and a disc golf tournament. Children's activities include games, demonstrations, and an acoustic family stage. The best part is, it's all for charity. The Springfield Service Organization for Humanitarian Opportunity (SOHO for short) is all about helping others through art and education, with ten charities chosen each year to split the proceeds from the event. More than $100,000 has been donated to local nonprofits since the festival began a decade ago.

Washington between Fifth and Sixth Streets, 815-348-7646,
www.springfieldsoho.org

WATCH LOCAL TALENT
AT THE LEGACY THEATRE

From the amusing antics of the Acro-Cats to the gritty, bold *Hedwig and the Angry Inch*, this local theater offers a variety of local talent, touring shows, concerts, and movies. If you're looking for entertainment with an edge, this is the place. If your tastes trend more toward ballet dancers and Gershwin, this is also your place. And the Sandbox Children's Theatre Company is a great way to introduce children to the arts.

101 E. Lawrence Ave., 217-528-9760,
www.atthelagacy.com

CARVE A PUMPKIN
FOR JACK-O-LANTERN SPECTACULAR

Bring the kids, sharpen your carving skills, and put some personality on those pumpkins! On the second weekend in October, area artists, students, and residents carve to their hearts content at the Carve for the Carillon fundraiser. The event is a prelude for the following weekend's Jack-O-Lantern Spectacular, when more than two-thousand hand-carved, illuminated jack-o-lanterns surround the park's botanical garden and carillon at Halloween.

1740 W. Fayette Ave., 217-546-3853,
www.carillon-rees.org

GET YOUR GROOVE ON
AT BEDROCK 66 CONCERTS

Bedrock 66 Live is a series of intimate concerts at local venues. What makes Bedrock 66 amazing is the caliber of talent it presents. You're liable to go see an unknown singer and then a month later spot her on a late-night talk show or in a *New York Times* article. Or you get to see the performer whose live music defined major events in your life. The acts range from folk and Americana to blues and rock—basically anything you could call "roots" music—and are recorded for later broadcast on public radio.

www.bedrock66.com

SEE THE CELESTIAL
AT UIS STAR PARTIES

Since 1980, more than one hundred twenty thousand people have taken advantage of this opportunity to look into the infinite. Experts explain stars, galaxies, stellar evolution, and how to identify stars and constellations, then help visitors use the telescopes at the University of Illinois at Springfield's observatory. The star parties take place on Fridays, but the university also arranges Sunday night events with special equipment for people with disabilities.

One University Plaza, 217-206-8342,
www.uis.edu

TIP
Call at 7 p.m. on the night of the party to see
if weather is suitable for viewing.

DANCE TO THE BLUES ON MONDAYS
AT THE ALAMO

The weekly blues session at The Alamo will make you forget it's a school night. Yes, you have to go to work the next day. Yes, you're usually in bed by the time the band starts its second set. But you might hear Reverend Raven and the Chain Smokin' Altar Boys or other local, national, and international artists, often passing through from Chicago and other larger cities. For three decades, Blue Monday, sponsored by the Illinois Central Blues Club, has given patrons proof for less than a $5 cover charge that the blues is alive and thriving here in Springfield. Come and see for yourself.

115 N. Fifth St., 217-523-1455,
www.alamospringfield.com

SCARE YOURSELF
ON A HAUNTED HAYRIDE

Bloodied bodies hanging from trees, chain-saw carrying madmen, and a good giggle now and then. It's all part of a haunted hayride at Carter Brothers. People of all ages wait in long lines for the chance to scare themselves silly every October at this seasonal family business, located on two-hundred acres of farmland near the Sangamon River. Take a seat in the back of the hay-filled wagon and travel through three miles of terror-filled special effects, live actors playing movie monsters, and things that go bump in the night. You can tour the haunted house while waiting for your turn on the wagon.

www.carterbroshauntedhayrides.com

LISTEN TO LOCAL JAZZ
AT ROBBIE'S

What better way to unwind after a week at work than kicking back with a few rounds with friends and listening to the Ed Clark Trio or Emerald Underground? A different act takes the stage each week at this small downtown eatery for Uptown Friday Night, sponsored by the Springfield Area Arts Council. Added bonus: no cover charge, but a 50/50 raffle is held to benefit the council's art programs.

4 S. Old State Capitol, 217-528-1901,
www.robbies.biz

KICK UP YOUR BOOTS
AT BOONDOCKS

If you like country music, and hey, even if you don't, Boondocks is the place to hear country acts that have hit the big time or are just about to: Florida Georgia Line, Kellie Pickler, Neal McCoy, Charlie Daniels. This nine-thousand-square-foot venue feels like the Astrodome, with more than enough space to kick up your heels. Even though it's new on the scene, it's packing in the young and rowdy, cowboy boot-wearing crowds. Not to mention it was named Academy of Country Music's Nightclub of the Year. The front bar opens at 6 p.m. on concert nights and venue doors open at 7 p.m. But prepare to prance around in your boots awhile, since headline acts don't start till around 10 p.m.

2909 N. Dirksen Parkway, 217-679-0145,
www.boondockspub.com

SPORTS AND RECREATION

PRACTICE PICKLEBALL
AT ILES PARK

It's easier than tennis—the ball is bigger, the rules are simpler, and you can learn to play in 10 minutes. What's not to love about pickleball? Wait, you don't know what it is? It's a paddle sport using a Wiffle-type ball hit over a low net. The president of the Springfield Pickleball Club describes it as "playing ping-pong standing on the table." Club members play daily during warm-weather months at eight regulation-sized courts at Iles Park. Anyone is welcome and membership fees are spent on court upkeep and equipment. A beginner class at Washington Park is available but not necessary. Just show up, grab a paddle, and learn to hit the ball.

Sixth and Iles streets, 217-415-9174,
www.facebook.com/springfieldpickleball

TRY YOUR HAND AT FRISBEE GOLF
AT LINCOLN PARK

If you think golf only involves a white ball and set of clubs, you should try it with a Frisbee—and this is the place to do it. The 18-hole course sits in a picturesque park with towering oak trees, a lagoon, and even some unexpected hills. It's the park district's largest course, measuring 6,422 linear feet, and offers challenging obstacles for all ages. So what are you waiting for?

1601 N. Fifth St., 217-753-2800,
www.springfieldparks.org

GO BIRDWATCHING
AT ADAMS WILDLIFE SANCTUARY

We know what you're thinking. Why go birdwatching in a busy, gritty residential area? But that's the beauty of the Margery Adams Wildlife Sanctuary—it's an oasis, forty acres of nature tucked away on the city's northwest side. In the spring when the wildflowers are in bloom, grab your binoculars and search for the eighty-one species of birds that have been identified there. You'll find plenty of benches along the quarter-mile Margery's Trail.

2315 Clear Lake Ave., 217-544-2473,
www.illinoisaudubon.org

RIDE THE TRAIL
AT RIVERSIDE STABLES

You don't even have to own a horse to enjoy an occasional trail ride. The folks at Riverside Stable will provide one and guide you on trails along the Sangamon River. Indulging your cowboy daydreams costs just $50 an hour. For the budding buckaroos, summer camps will teach them the basics of horsemanship like how to groom, saddle, and ride, as well as how to determine horse breeds, colors and markings like a true horseman. The lessons are mixed with typical camp activities like swimming, crafts, games and hayrack rides. The stable also offers experienced riders a place to board their horse. When you get off the saddle, see the scenic area via water in a canoe or kayak, which can be rented on site. Facilities are also available for private parties or field trips.

2310 Chinchilla Ln., 217-522-7702,
www.riversidestable.com

WATCH THE JR. BLUES
TAKE THE ICE

Grab a blanket and a warm coat and head to the Nelson Center on a Saturday night to watch the boys in blue take to the ice. The Jr. Blues are a Tier II junior ice hockey team in the North American Hockey League's Midwest Division. The atmosphere is up close and personal, and fans get a great bird's-eye view of the fast-paced action. How can you not love a team with a skating blue gill as the mascot?

Lincoln Park, 1601 N. Fifth St., 217-525-2589,
www.jrblues.com

VOLUNTEER TO WALK A DOG
AT APL

Taking a dog for a walk is fun, right? Walking a dog that lives in a shelter, awaiting a forever home is even better. At the Animal Protective League, you can volunteer to help in lots of ways, from cleaning cat beds to serving up chilli at the annual fundraiser. But getting some exercise and giving adoptable dogs a chance to stretch their legs in some one-on-one social time is a win-win. All that's required is a brief training session and a little goodwill. You might meet a new four-legged friend. APL is open to volunteers every day, year-round, from 8:30 a.m. to 5 p.m.

1001 Taintor Road, 217-544-7387,
www.apl-shelter.org.

PADDLE DOWN
THE SANGAMON RIVER

This isn't white-water rafting; it's an easy, gentle paddling adventure. The most excitement you might have is seeing a blue heron sitting on a log. But that's OK, because it's all about serenity and turning off your brain, while you paddle the eight-mile stretch from Wheeling Park in Riverton to Riverside Park. The water is low during the summer, and sandbars provide good rest stops. Riverside Stables will rent canoes for you and shuttle you from Riverside to Wheeling Park, even if you bring your own boat.

1601 N. Fifth St., 215-247-0417,
fow.org

You can rent kayaks and canoes at several locations:

Lake Springfield Marina
17 Water's Edge Blvd., 217-483-3625,
www.lakespringfieldmarina.com

Riverside Stables
2310 Chinchilla Ln., 217-522-7702,
www.riversidestable.com

Lincoln's New Salem Canoe Rental
15588 History Ln., Petersburg, 217-494-3957,

HEY, FIDO!

Hey Fido! Do you want to go to the park, run around like crazy, sniff out some new friends, and mark our territory? Me too! Let's get our humans to take us to Stuart Park, where we can burn off energy in the large fenced dog run area while the humans sit and watch under the shelter. And those petite poodle types can stay in the nearby small dog pen—you know how they are.

1800 Winch Ln., 217-544-1751,
www.springfieldparks.org

STOP AND SMELL THE ROSES
AT WASHINGTON PARK
BOTANICAL GARDEN

Near the top of this 150-acre park, with its immense trees, picnic areas, tennis courts, nature trails, fishing ponds, and a lagoon full of fowl, sits the crown jewel: the Botanical Garden. A glass-domed Conservatory that houses more than 150 species of tropical and exotic plants is the place to linger during cold winter months. But in spring and summer, the place you want to soak up sun is in the collection of 10 gardens surrounding the Conservatory, filled with roses, peonies, iris, scent-and-texture plants for the visually impaired, perennials, cacti, and shade plants. The tiered Rose Garden, complete with arbors and benches to sit and breathe in the beauty, is a popular place for summer weddings. There's also a rockery and greenhouse with seasonal displays like Easter lilies and orchids.

1740 W. Fayette Ave., 217-546-4116,
www.springfieldparks.org/facilities/botanicalGardens/

• •

SAVOR THE SERENITY
OF LINCOLN MEMORIAL GARDENS

This sanctuary designed by internationally known landscape architect Jens Jensen honors Abraham Lincoln by recreating the woodland and prairie landscape Lincoln knew during his years in central Illinois. Six miles of wood chip hiking trails snake through one hundred acres along the shore of Lake Springfield, all planted with native trees, wildflowers, and prairie plants. Eight stone council rings and wooden benches carved with Lincoln quotes scattered throughout the area offer peaceful resting and reflection spots. The site also includes a handicapped-accessible interpretive trail. While the serene area attracts birdwatchers, photographers, artists, nature enthusiasts, and school children year round, special events like Maple Syrup Time and Indian Summer Festival celebrate the seasons, and there are summer ecology and naturalist camps for kids. Take note that the garden is not a public park, so no bikes, pets, or alcohol are permitted.

2301 E. Lake Dr., 217-529-1111,
www.lincolnmemorialgarden.org

TAKE A SPIN ON THE ICE
AT THE NELSON CENTER

Whether you need to practice your double axel or just learn to stand up without falling, the Nelson Center is the place for you. The Lincoln Park facility has two indoor ice rinks, six locker rooms, and two concession areas. It offers lessons in basic skating, figure skating, and hockey and provides rental skates. Since it houses the only two indoor ice rinks within a 60-mile radius, it serves as home base for most area ice related programs, events and activities. Even if you don't take classes, open time is scheduled each week so the community can take a spin on the ice just for the fun of it. And better yet, the fun doesn't end when the weather heats up. This year-round facility can be enjoyed during the dog days of summer too. The Nelson Center pool, a seasonal outdoor aquatic facility, is open between Memorial Day and Labor Day weekends. Take a turn on the slide or let the little ones splash in a separate kiddy pool.

Lincoln Park, 1601 N. Fifth St., 217-753-2800,
www.springfieldparks.org

TOSS A BOCCE BALL
AT OBED AND ISAAC'S

This pub's beer garden is like a playground for adults, with a cozy fire pit, plenty of picnic tables, and four bag game sets. But you've got to try bocce ball. After all, it's just some big colored balls being thrown in some sand, how hard can it be? Well, even if you don't have the required skill, strategy, or luck, go ahead and give it a try, because nobody here cares how good you are. Just know that after a few Obed's Pride amber ales, it may get harder.

500 S. Sixth St., 217-670-0627,
www.connshospitalitygroup.com

SPEND A DAY
AT THE RACES
AT THE ILLINOIS STATE FAIR

Sure, the Illinois State Fair is loads of fun, but sometimes it's nice to take a break from the corn dogs and butter cows. So how about spending a sunny afternoon watching beautiful horses while sipping a cold one in the shade of the Grandstand? This is harness racing, where horses, running at a controlled pace rather than a gallop, pull drivers in small carts. Place a few smart bets and you might win back your beer money.

801 E. Sangamon Ave., 217-782-6661,
www.illinois.gov/statefair

PEDAL THE
LOST BRIDGE TRAIL

There's no prettier place to take your bicycle for a spin than the Lost Bridge Trail, a five-mile stretch from the east side of town to Rochester. The popular multi-use trail, built on the old Baltimore and Ohio Railroad line, starts behind the Illinois Department of Transportation building. A canopy of trees provides good shade along most of the trail, and a sweet treat awaits you at the end—hand-dipped ice cream at Cocoa Blue, a Rochester chocolate shop. Ample parking is available on the IDOT building grounds for access to the westerly end of the trail. Easy access is also available just off Route 29 at Hilltop Road and in the town of Rochester.

2300 Dirksen Parkway parking lot,
www.springfieldparks.org/parks/bikeTrails/LostBridge.aspx

TIP

The Springfield Park District
The Springfield Park District manages an extensive trail system that connects Springfield to several surrounding communities. The trails are open to walkers, runners, bicyclists, rollerbladers, strollers, people in wheelchairs, and cross-country skiers.

GO SLEDDING
AT CENTENNIAL PARK

So it's a snow day. Don't just sit there watching the flakes fall. Hit the hills and go sledding! Centennial Park is home to a one hundred-foot man-made hill. It's not Mount Everest, but it's the largest hill in the area and will provide plenty of sliding fun. Another option: Pasfield Golf Course, a popular hill near Washington Park, at 1700 W. Lawrence Ave.

5751 Bunker Hill Road, New Berlin; 217-698-6049,
www.springfieldparks.org

CAST A LINE
AT SANGCHRIS LAKE STATE PARK

This is an angler's paradise, stocked with largemouth bass, bluegill, crappie, channel and flathead catfish, bullhead, and carp. You can obtain statewide and site regulations on size and creel limits at the park office. Also great for boating, hunting, or family gatherings, Sangchris Lake provides an abundance of recreational opportunities amid native forests of oak, maple, butternut, and persimmon. Totaling more than three thousand acres and offering one hundred and twenty miles of shoreline, the park got its unusual name because it extends into both Sangamon and Christian counties. You can camp here but a couple tiny cabins offer a more comfortable option.

9898 Cascade Rd., Rochester, 217-498-9208

SEE
A SLIDERS BALLGAME

Nothing says summertime better than a night at the ballpark, hot dog and beverage in hand, watching the batter up. The Springfield Sliders, minor league members of the summer collegiate baseball wood bat Prospect League, play at Robin Roberts Stadium. With giveaways, promotions, and entertainment between innings— and, of course, Speedy the mascot—a game here is more than just baseball. And if watching from the stands isn't enough, you can buy the $159 "Be a Slider for the Day" package, which lets you take batting practice with the team, wear a team uniform, throw out or catch the ceremonial first pitch, and watch the game from the dugout.

1415 N. Grand Ave. E., 217-679-3511,
www.springfieldsliders.com

TIP

On your way to the game, stop by Krekel's Custard and Hamburgers for a burger and milkshake. Burgers are flat in the best kind of 'smashed on a sizzling griddle' kind of way with crispy edges, and ice cream shakes come in 16 flavors including lemon and root beer.

2121 N. Grand Ave. E., 217-525-4952, www.krekelscustard.com

Photo credit: Christopher Wills

CULTURE AND HISTORY

GET A MILITARY BRIEFING
AT THE ILLINOIS STATE MILITARY MUSEUM

This museum is small but mighty. Let's start with the exterior. The imposing, stone, castle-like building surrounded by a barbed wire metal fence means business. The helicopter with painted grinning shark teeth, next to the massive M-47 tank in the parking lot reinforces that image. But inside, this museum tells the solemn, personal story of the citizen soldier in Illinois, from the Revolutionary War to today's war on terror, through weapons, uniforms and photographs on display. You'll see an Illinois Civil War regimental flag, an 1883 Gatling Gun and pictures of Illinoisans killed in the Gulf War, along with personal artifacts and notes left by their families. And the weirdest, must-see highlights are the wooden leg of Mexican General Santa Anna and a board Lincoln used for target practice. Free admission.

1301 N. MacArthur Blvd., 217-761-3910,
www.il.ngb.army.mil/Heritage/Museum.aspx

TAKE YOUR MEDICINE
AT THE PEARSON MUSEUM

The medical profession is ever-changing, as evidenced by the exhibits of the Pearson Museum at Southern Illinois University. Dedicated to preserving the evolution of all forms of medicine, "the Pearson Museum collects, preserves, and interprets the history of medicine, health care, nursing, dentistry, and pharmacy from all cultures and eras, but with particular emphasis on the Midwest and the Mississippi River basin" according to the SIU website. Along with a large collection of medical textbooks and exhibits showcasing medical breakthroughs that have enhanced our lives, the museum provides outreach programs to schools and other interested groups in and around Springfield. Mixing the weird with the wonderful, the Pearson displays replicas of a 19th century doctor's office and a Depression-era drugstore. At any given time, it might display scary-looking medical instruments of the past or the pills and tonics once peddled by quacks. The museum is only open to the public by appointment. Admission is free but donations are accepted.

801 N. Rutledge St., 217-545-2155,
www.siumed.edu/medhum/2010Templates/2010Pearson/
2010PearsonIndex.html

PRETEND TO BE A PIONEER
AT CLAYVILLE

Walking the grounds of the Clayville Historic Site transports you back nearly 200 years. Its 14 acres include the state's second-oldest brick building, the Broadwell Inn and Tavern, built in 1824 as a stagecoach stop. It also has two 1830s log cabins and a blacksmith shop. Although the Clayville's staff offers unique, custom-tailored programs on pioneer life for school groups, they also host annual weekend events like the Fall Festival, Folk Music Festival, and a Clayville Christmas. This once-neglected property, listed in 1930 on the Historic American Buildings Registry, was brought back to life by the Pleasant Plains Historical Society.

12828 Illinois Route 125, Pleasant Plains, 217-481-4430,
www.clayville.org

EXPERIENCE HISTORY
AT THE AFRICAN-AMERICAN MUSEUM

After visiting Lincoln's final resting place, stop at the small stone building just outside the gates of Oak Ridge Cemetery for a history lesson on the region's African-American citizens. The Springfield and Central Illinois African-American History Museum mixes historical exhibits, modern artwork, and photographs to tell its story. *Journey on the Road to Freedom* follows the life of African-Americans from the time of slavery through the abolitionist movement, Civil War, and signing of the Emancipation Proclamation. One wall is dedicated to images from a prominent local photographer who used his lens to capture national figures—like Dr. Martin Luther King and Fats Domino—during his fifty-year career working for a state official. The most poignant are the honest glimpses of the daily life of local citizens dancing in the street, and at work in a greenhouse and general store. Ask the museum staff about walking tours, including key sites from the 1908 riots that tore the city apart.

1440 Monument Ave., 217-391-6323,
www.spiaahfmuseum.org

TIP
Stop by the Lincoln Souvenir and Gift Shop that's been a fixture near the cemetery entrance since the 1930s, for your fill of Lincoln busts and shiny copper pennies.

PAUSE FOR POETRY
AT THE VACHEL LINDSAY HOME

Visit poet Vachel Lindsay's home for a poetry reading. The "prairie troubadour," artist, film critic, and poet received national acclaim during the early 1900s with poems such as "On the Building of Springfield" and "Abraham Lincoln Walks at Midnight," which describes Lincoln's mystical return to his old stomping grounds. The home, originally owned by Mary Lincoln's sister, is yet another tie to the Lincoln family. But instead of walking through yet another historic home, here you can enjoy a little culture while seeing the home where the poet was born (and met a grisly end). Hear a nationally known poet perform a written work at one of the "Poets in the Parlor" reading series, or attend an open-mic night where local authors get a shot at reading their original prose. There are seasonal hours.

603 S. Fifth St., 217-524-0901,
www.vachellindsay.org

EXPLORE SPRINGFIELD HISTORY
AT THE ELIJAH ILES HOUSE

Tour one of the city's oldest homes, and you can almost see Abraham Lincoln playing cards in the front parlor of this charming white cottage. He was a frequent visitor to the Greek Revival style structure with a large front porch that was home to many interesting residents, from merchants and solders to politicians and women leaders. You'll learn secrets of the home, like its move across town and why the ceiling is painted blue. Its namesake—one of the city's founding fathers—also built the city's first store and is sometimes called the "Father of Springfield." The interior features original walnut woodwork, period furnishings, and a graceful staircase. A city museum in the basement includes local history and a fun Illinois Watches exhibit. Open for tours from 12–4 p.m. Wednesdays and Saturdays. Admission is free, but a $3 donation is suggested.

628 S. Seventh St., 217-492-5929,
www.iles-house.blogspot.com

ENJOY THE HOLIDAYS
AT THE DANA-THOMAS HOUSE

This 1902 house is the work of Frank Lloyd Wright, who, at the time, was a young man breaking new ground in what would come to be known as the Prairie School of architecture. It features more of Wright's specially designed furniture, lights, and art glass than any other home in America, making it a wonder any time of year. But walk through it during the holidays, when it's decorated with subtle, imaginative greenery, lit by the soft glow of candles and filled with the sound of holiday music, and you will experience the full magnitude of Wright's innovative designs.

301 E. Lawrence Ave., 217-782-6776,
www.dana-thomas.org

GET GOOSEBUMPS
ON A HAUNTED SPRINGFIELD TOUR

Do you believe in ghosts? You might after learning about Springfield's spooky side and haunted history. Based on availability, the tour guide takes visitors to sites believed to be inhabited by things that go bump in the night. You'll explore a hidden cemetery, hear about who haunts a local theater, and even engage in a light paranormal investigation. Bring your camera and an open mind.

217-502-8687,
www.springfieldwalks.com

TIP
Other summer and fall tours including the Prohibition Pub Crawl and Lincoln's Ghost Walk: Legends and Lore.

ENJOY PORK AND POTTERY
FOR ART AT SAA

Eat pork, paint a pot, support art—what could be simpler? Roasted: Hot Pots and Pork is an event that lets you decorate your own piece of pottery and then watch it fire in an outdoor kiln, while feasting on locally prepared whole hog pork barbecue. You don't need an art degree or skilled hand to enjoy this casual, family-friendly fundraiser for the Springfield Art Association (SAA). The outdoor event, on the lawn of the association's headquarters next to a community garden, lets kids of all ages explore their creative side. To top it off, an art auction gives you a chance to bid on paper-mâché pigs given lavish makeovers by local celebrities and artists. The pigs are located at businesses around town before the event and go home with new owners after dinner.

700 N. 4th St., 217-523-2631,
www.springfieldart.org

BE ARTFULLY INSPIRED
AT THE PHARMACY

Skip the dinner and movie on a Friday night and indulge your artsy side. Go to an art exhibit opening reception at The Pharmacy Art and Gallery Space, have a glass of wine, and mingle with the artists who created the work. The gallery, which got its name from a former location in an old drug store, is right at home in a former 1920s Cadillac dealership with soaring ceilings and bright white walls—the perfect backdrop for the ever-evolving artwork. You might see a boat-sized bird's nest made from nature's materials outside in the parking lot, or a collection of pastel paintings of poppies. This space not only celebrates the area's multi-dimensional artists, but also hosts poetry readings, films, music, and other special events. This is the perfect place to view and buy art with the cool crowd. In addition to special evening reception hours, the gallery is open during regular hours 12–6 p.m. Thursday through Saturday.

711 S. Fifth St., 801-810-9278,
www.pharmacygallery.com

LEARN SAFETY
AT THE ILLINOIS FIRE MUSEUM

Who hasn't dreamed of being a firefighter at one time or another? This small but mighty museum in a former fire station at the state fairgrounds houses a vast array of antique and modern firefighting equipment. There's plenty to see, from fire safety exhibits to a collection of firefighter squad patches from all over the world to photos of famous Illinois fires. The kids will love the 1857 horse-drawn, hand-pumped water wagon. Free admission. Open during the State Fair; otherwise, call for appointment.

Building #7, Central Ave. and Main Street, Illinois State Fairgrounds,
217-785-7487,
www.sfm.illinois.gov/public/Illinois-Fire-Museum

REMEMBER THE WAR
AT THE DAUGHTERS OF UNION VETERANS OF THE CIVIL WAR MUSEUM

You might be surprised to learn that Springfield is the national headquarters for the Daughters of Union Veterans of the Civil War (or DUVCW to its friends). The organization has a small but fascinating museum here, with glass cases containing countless artifacts of Civil War history, like a copy of a famous letter from Abraham Lincoln to a mother who lost five sons in battle or a sewing kit with thread made from horse hair. Kids will get a kick out of holding the cannon balls or admiring the hand carved chess set made by a soldier waiting to go into battle. Other artifacts include a preserved hand-beaded black mourning dress and a quilt stitched from silk convention ribbons. Open 9:30 a.m–3:30 p.m. Tuesday through Saturday. Free admission. Library open by appointment.

503 S. Walnut St., 217-544-0616,
www.duvcw.org

DRIVE
THE MOTHER ROAD

The Mother Road. Main Street of America. US Route 66. Take the battered blacktop from the north side of Springfield to a section near Auburn that is still paved with brick. (It's on the National Register of Historic Places and makes a great photo op!) If you own a convertible, this is the time to break it out. The road will twist and turn a few times, so you might want check out online maps like the ones at www.RoadTrippers.com or www.Historic66.com. Watch for markers along the route, but don't worry if you get a little lost. That's part of the fun, and you'll still get your kicks.

866-378-7866,
www.illinoisroute66.org

TIP

Have your picture taken with the giant bearded fiberglass Muffler Man at Lauterbach Tire and Auto Service on Wabash, then stop for a lunch at the Cozy Dog Drive-in, the original hot-dog-on-a-stick joint (it's a corn dog in other places, but here the PC term is "cozy dog"). Check out the memorabilia and photo albums, sign the guest book, and take a selfie with the life-sized Pronto Pup prop

1569 Wabash Ave, 217-546-2600,
www.lauterbachtire.com
2935 S. 6th St., 217-525-1992,
ww.cozydogdrivein.com

EXPAND YOUR HORIZONS
WITH ACADEMY OF LIFELONG LEARNING

Want to make new friends, try golf, or maybe watch an old movie? The Academy of Lifelong Learning (ALL), a service of Lincoln Land Community College, gives people over fifty a chance to learn new things and be more active, proving that life just keeps getting better with age. This senior-focused group offers up to twelve opportunities each month to meet people and have fun, from day trips to technology training. If you prefer something a little more relaxed, monthly breakfast meetings at a local cafeteria feature guest speakers. Or if bicycling, bowling, or reading books is your thing, there are special groups for that too.

5250 Shepherd Rd., 217-786-2432,
www.llcc.edu/community-education/academy-lifelong-learning/

FOLLOW A TOUR
OF PLACES AND EVENTS
THAT SPARKED THE BIRTH OF THE NAACP

Springfield was torn apart in 1908, when white mobs burned black-owned homes and businesses, and lynched two people. Black citizens responded by arming themselves and shooting several attackers. It took the state militia to restore order, but the events helped galvanize the African-American community to form the NAACP. Students of the people's history can follow the markers at key points around Springfield on this self-guided walking tour to learn the lessons of this sad story, including dedicated grave markers of four riot victims and markers commemorating eight downtown riot sites. Then view the sculpture next to the Abraham Lincoln Presidential Library and Museum that serves as a memorial. Get a map and brochure at the Springfield Convention and Visitors Bureau, 109 N. Seventh Street.

217-789-2360,
www.visitspringfieldillinois.com

Photo credit: Christopher Wills

TAKE IN THE BEAUTY
OF THE STATE CAPITOL

Stop by the State Capitol building not only to watch Illinois politicians in action from the balcony, but to soak in the artwork, statues, murals, and beautiful architectural design of the limestone Italian Renaissance Revival building. It's a beauty, inside and out. Don't forget to gaze up at the ceiling of stained glass that makes up the inner dome and the statues of famous Illinoisans on the corbels beneath it. It's even taller than the Capitol in Washington, D.C., making it unique compared to other state capitols in the US. Free tours are given every half hour from 8 a.m.–4 p.m., except from 12–1 p.m., on weekdays, and every hour from 9 a.m.–3 p.m., except from 12–1 p.m., on weekends. Go during the week if you want to see government in action.

Capitol Avenue and Second Street, 217-782-2099,
www.ilstatehouse.com

LAND OF LINCOLN

VISIT THE LINCOLN HOME
NATIONAL HISTORIC SITE

If you have limited time but want to experience a bit of Lincoln history, this site should top your list. The buff-colored, two-story Greek Revival house is where Abraham Lincoln and his wife Mary Todd Lincoln lived before he became President of the United States in 1861. The house, part of a larger area designated as a National Historic Site run by the National Park Service, is the perfect place to get a glimpse inside the life of the man who led the nation through the Civil War. Beware that tours of the home fill up quickly during the busy summer season, so it's a good idea to get tickets early in the day so you don't miss out.

TIP

Admission is free, but you need a ticket from the Visitor Center located on the grounds of the park for the tour. Save time to wander around the restored, four-block, 19th century neighborhood, complete with wooden walkways and gaslights.

426 S. Seventh St., 217-391-3221,
www.nps.gov/liho

RUB THE STATUE'S NOSE
AT LINCOLN'S TOMB

This tomb is the final resting place of Lincoln, his wife, and three of their four sons. Outside, it's a soaring, 117-foot obelisk adorned with a statue of Lincoln and sculptures representing branches of the military. Inside are two marble chambers, one of which contains the crypts for Lincoln's family and the stone marking where Lincoln's body lies deep below ground, forever safe from grave robbers. Because it contains Lincoln's Tomb and state memorials to troops from World War II, Korea, and Vietnam, Oak Ridge Cemetery is surpassed only by Arlington National Cemetery as the most-visited cemetery in the nation.

1500 Monument Ave., 217-782-2717,
www.lincolntomb.org

TIP
Don't forget to rub the nose of the bronze Lincoln bust at the tomb's entrance. It's supposed to bring you good luck.

TOUR
THE OLD STATE CAPITOL

You can take a 30-minute guided tour of the place where President Lincoln spent time as a state legislator, gave his famous "House Divided" speech, and managed his transition from candidate to president. Or you can walk around on your own, soaking in the ambiance, from the antique desks and wood-burning stoves to the dramatic staircase and massive architectural columns, meticulously recreated to resemble the 1860s. You can almost hear President Lincoln making a speech here or picture local citizens paying their final respects to the assassinated leader before his burial. Tour guides are more than happy to answer questions. Take time to walk around the exterior, which is worth a stop just for its beauty and location in the heart of downtown. The two-story National Historic Landmark is also home to the Illinois Visitors Center, with information on local and statewide sites.

1 Old State Capitol Plaza, 217-785-7960,
swww.illinoishistory.gov

TIP
Visit during the annual Civil War Encampment for an authentic outdoor living history lesson with music, demonstrations, and exhibits.

EXPERIENCE
THE ABRAHAM LINCOLN PRESIDENTIAL LIBRARY AND MUSEUM

If you can only do one Lincoln-related thing, this is it. The museum displays one-of-a-kind Lincoln artifacts, re-creates key moments from his life (a slave auction is particularly haunting), and uses special effects to tell Lincoln's story in innovative ways. Don't miss the "Ghosts of the Library" show, which will leave you mystified as to what was real and what wasn't, and the Whispering Gallery will give you a new insight into the abuse Lincoln endured. Stop by the Treasures Gallery with its ever-changing array of artifacts and you might see Lincoln's stovepipe hat, the toy cannon his children played with, or a copy of the Gettysburg Address. This is a spot where you will want to spend several hours and visit more than once.

112 N. Sixth St., 217-558-8844,
www.presidentlincoln.org,
www.alplm.org

LOOK FOR LINCOLN
ON A HISTORY HUNT

Like a challenge? Go on a history hunt by looking for exhibits explaining Abraham Lincoln's life and times in Springfield. The "Looking for Lincoln" project hosts 40 wayside exhibits which serve as big informational postcards about the people, places, and events that impacted Lincoln's life. You can be walking along and suddenly discover you're at the location where Lincoln played handball, or Mary bought sugar on credit. You can stand on the same downtown corner where in 1860 stood a "wigwam," a makeshift gathering place with a sawdust floor and wooden benches for Springfield Republicans.

Throughout the Abraham Lincoln National Heritage Area, 217-782-6817, www.lookingforlincoln.com

TIP
Be a total tourist and collect a rubbing of every medallion on each of the blue-trimmed signs. Just bring a pencil and piece of paper to get a souvenir symbolizing each story as you explore the spots where history happened.

ENJOY
UNION SQUARE PARK

After you visit the Abraham Lincoln Presidential Library and Museum across the street, take a rest in this 86,000-square-foot urban park. If you're lucky, you'll catch one of the many popular free activities, like a performance by the 33rd Illinois Volunteer Regiment Band, a Civil War reenactment group, or a local production of the musical *The Civil War*. View two Abe Lincoln statues as you meander among the climbing roses, Mary Todd daylilies, flowering dogwoods, and beautiful landscaping.

212 N. Sixth St., 217-558-8844,
www.presidentlincoln.org

More Lincoln sites:

Union Station–Lincoln:
From History to Hollywood
500 E. Madison St., 800-610-2094,
www.presidentlincoln.illinois.gov

Lincoln Depot
930 East Monroe Street, 217-544-8695,
www.lincolndepot.org

Lincoln Family Pew
First Presbyterian Church, 321 S. Seventh St.,
217-528-4311,
www.lincolnschurch.org

Lincoln Ledger
Lobby, Chase Bank, Sixth and Washington Streets,
217-527-3860,
www.abrahamlincolnonline.org

SHOPPING AND FASHION

Photo credit: Penny Zimmerman-Wills

PAINT YOUR OWN POT
AT CHARTRUSE

It's hard to miss this Pepto-pink shop, which is the perfect backdrop for the brightly hued flower pots, jewelry, pet bowls, and platters. It's fun to browse the rustic cabinets filled with pottery – from key chains and coffee mugs to wine coolers and heart pendants hanging from leather ropes. All the ceramics are painted in the shop owner's signature design – bright hues with splatters of color and black and white accents, in a weathered glaze. But the back half of the shop is where you can indulge your inner Picasso, with shelves of unfinished bisque ware waiting to be brought to life at the large wood tables where up to 30 people take classes. The number of classes varies according to the season, but usually two classes a month are offered. The informal setting is the perfect place to make your own vintage inspired ceramic holiday tree or large floral garden stake.

229 S. Sixth St., 217-891-6990,
www.chartruse.net

SHOP
SIXTH STREET

An eclectic mix of art galleries, retail shops, antique stores, and restaurants make the downtown Sixth Street area a fun, convenient shopping destination. Take a break from touring the Lincoln sites and enjoy a day of retail therapy. Don't miss the rotating fine art exhibits at the SAA Collective, located in the Hoogland Center for the Arts, or the selection of locally made jewelry, art, photography, and vintage collections at The Roost and Urban Sassafras. If you like to wear your humor on your feet, check out the large sock collection at the Cardologist, a funky card and gift shop. If you're in the market for a Lincoln souvenir, Old Capitol Goods has everything from bronze busts and political figure bobble-heads to a large selection of Lincoln themed T-shirts. And don't forget to refuel with a personal-sized pizza, homemade pie and coffee at Andiamo.

Here are some shops to check out:

SAA Collective
in the Hoogland Center for the Arts
420 S. Sixth St., 217-544-2787, www.springfieldart.org

Chartruse
229 S. Sixth St., 217-891-6990

Studio on 6th Street
215 S. Sixth St., 217-522-8006, www.studioon6thart.com

Murphy's Loft
210 S. Sixth St., 217-744-7225, www.murphys-loft.com

The Roost
216 S. Sixth St., 217-528-2234, www.theroostcoop.com

Andiamo
204 S. Sixth St., 217-523-3262, www.cafeandiamo.com

Urban Sassafras
104 N. Sixth St., 217-210-2303, www.urbansassafras.com

Wild Rose
115 N. Sixth St., 217-572-1884,

Abe's Old Hat Antiques
111 N. Sixth St., 217-414-3320, www.abesoldhatantiques.com

Old Capitol Goods
2 S. Old State Capitol Plaza, 217-525-1825, www.oldcapitolgoods.com

Merchant House
625 E. Monroe St., 217-744-3735, www.merchanthouse.net

The Cardologist
627 E. Adams St., 217-525-4121

SPEND A DAY
HUNTING FOR ANTIQUES

Love to dig through dusty piles of old stuff? We've got you covered. Abe's Old Hat Antiques is an intimate downtown shop full of antiques and collectibles, including Civil War and Americana products, advertising signs, and folk art. Then head to Springfield Vintage, specializing in items from the 1940s-70s, where you'll find all the things to make your pad groovy, from pastel Pyrex and hanging swag lamps, to retro barware, and racks of retro clothing to blend in to your new surroundings. The Sangamon Antique Mall, a three-floor, 20,000-square-foot building, is filled with enough tchotchkes, kitsch, and cool antiques to bring you back again, just to see what's new. The best digging is on the third floor, where things are less arranged and a little dustier. Just a 20-minute drive out of town, Lisa's Antique Malls I and II offer two buildings and 40,000 square feet of stuff, just a half-mile from each other. More treasures can be found at the Springfield and Barrel antique malls. On your way back to town, swing by Again, a charming shop down a long country lane full of fun 50s furniture, primitives, and more. Treat yourself to a whole day.

Springfield Vintage
501 W. Monroe St., 217-652-8413

Abe's Old Hat Antiques
111 N. Sixth St., 217-414-3320,
www.abesoldhatantiques.com

Sangamon Antique Mall
3050 E. Sangamon Ave., 217-522-7740,

Lisa's I Antique Mall
14266 Frazee Road, Divernon, 217-628-1111,
www.lisasantiquemalls.com

Lisa's II Antique Mall
490 W. State, Route 104, Divernon, 217-628-3333,
www.lisasantiquemalls.com

Springfield Antique Mall
3031 Reilly Dr., 217-522-3031

The Barrel Antique Mall
5850 S. Sixth Street Rd., 217-585-1438,
www.barrelantiquemall.com

Again
2776 Ostermeier Road, Chatham, 217-652-6887

FIND FASHION FOR LESS
AT CONSIGNMENT SHOPS

Second-hand. Pre-owned. Slightly used. Whatever term you use, scoring a $120 designer jacket for $20 in your size makes your heart sing. The number of consignment and resale shops is growing because who doesn't love a bargain? Two to check out are Second Time Around, where you might find a Coach purse or leather boots, and The Clothing Rack, where $20 can buy just-like-new costume jewelry.

Second Time Around
2440 Denver Dr., 217-744-7873

Consign & Design
2412 Denver Dr., 217-528-4723

Cindy's Just Kids
2412 Denver Dr., 217-525-3800

The Clothing Rack
271 S. Sherman Blvd., Suites B & C, Sherman,
217-496-3633

Remarkable Resale
130 S. John St., Rochester, 217-498-9434,
www.remarkableresale.com

STEP BACK IN TIME
AT THE VILLAGE HOMESTEAD

A cluster of about 10 tiny buildings, including an antique store and octagonal shed, make up this charmingly manicured village within the town of Kilbourne, population 300, located about 40 miles northwest of Springfield. What started as one woman's dream has been carried on by friends and family after her death. The buildings were mostly found in the surrounding countryside, then moved to the site and rebuilt. You can buy primitive antiques and locally handcrafted items like barnwood garden trellises.

206 S. First St., Route 97, Kilbourne, 309-538-4451

BUY LOCAL ART
AT THE ROOST

This cozy artist co-op is the place to find an original steampunk pigeon painting or a hand-beaded bracelet. A soaring ceiling covered in vintage ceiling tin, bright front windows and barn wood covered walls form the backdrop for an array of locally, handmade gifts and home décor. From a large wall-sized painting to the tiniest metal earrings, this is the place to go for a unique gift. Jewelry, garden art, knitwear, bath products, photography, handcrafted wood items, wall art, and vintage goods are made and curated by 30 local artists and craftsmen. A special corner in the back features upcycled, vintage and children's clothing and accessories. Special events might include a visit from a local author and her miniature horse. The shop's quirky vibe and penchant for chickens is evident by a sampling of bird-related items including key chains, egg-shaped bath bombs, and a collection of vintage chicken pictures adorning the wall.

216 S. 6th St., 217-528-2234,
www.theroostcoop.com

WATCH ART BEING CREATED
AT URBAN SASSAFRAS

Located next door to the Abraham Lincoln Presidential Library, this inspired shop celebrates art, whether it's fine art photography, original paintings, jewelry, repurposed vintage goods, or modern mixed media. The walls are lined with black and white photographs in barn wood frames, bright pastel paintings and upcycled items like coat hooks made from worn bicycle seats. Painted and repurposed furniture form vignettes among the artwork, from a handcrafted patio table made from industrial piping and a rustic wood spool, to a white vintage dresser given a dose of romance with a handwritten French poem. The shop is ever-changing, and you might find delicate sea shells holding air plants hanging from the ceilings, or playful wall lights made from a jumble of doll parts, toy animals and wooden boxes on the walls. Stop in for a cup of coffee and watch an artist at work in the shop's open studio. Wee ones are welcome, too, with a whimsical children's merchandise section, a play table with craft supplies so kids can play while their parents shop, and monthly children's art classes.

100 N. 6th St., 217-210-2303,
www.urbansassafras.com

ENJOY LOCAL DELIGHTS
AT PEASE'S AT BUNN GOURMET

When two of the city's oldest companies join forces, it's a delight for the taste buds and for the eyes. Step inside and you're greeted by over-the-top crystal chandeliers, soaring walls filled with jars of pastel candies, and a glass-enclosed candy kitchen. You can buy Pease's famous confections, like Lincoln Logs (chocolate covered pretzel sticks), truffles and dark chocolate almond clusters, as well as a selection of local products like coffee, beer salt and Bunn Farms beef. An adjoining café offers a limited lunch menu, wine, ice cream and homemade baked goods like cheesecake, cookies and fruit tarts. Order soup and a slice of quiche (but save room for dessert), take a seat on the couch by the fireplace and just enjoy. Toast on the Terrace events are held Thursday evenings with live music on the patio and handcrafted cocktails.

2941 Plaza Dr., 217-793-1840,
www.bunngourmet.com

RELISH RETAIL THERAPY
AT THE GABLES

Spend a leisurely afternoon at this upscale shopping complex on the city's west side, which mixes traditional apparel stores like Talbots, Chico's, Apricot Lane, and Jos. A. Bank with local businesses like Westside Stories, Jim Wilson Interiors, Homescapes, Earthen Pottery & Boutique, and Sarah Petty Photography. An art fair held at the complex each summer is a great time to buy local art and score some bargains at sidewalk sales. Stop at McCormick's Smokehouse for mouth-watering brisket or get sushi and drinks at Pao Bistro, which offers a luscious libations menu, from champagne coulis to martinis to mojitos.

2808 Plaza Dr., 217-793-3344,
www.thegablesofspringfield.com

McCormick's, 2930 Plaza Dr., 217-793-1183,
www.mccormicksrestaurant.net

Pao Bistro, 2824 Plaza Dr., 217-546-4660,
www.paobistro.com

REFRESH YOUR HOME
WITH FURNITURE FROM MAGNOLIA LANE

If your style is more urban farmhouse, but your furniture screams "Grandma's basement," Magnolia Lane can help with that. This large store is the best of both worlds: discounted new furniture from a major department store; returns, floor models, and overstock; and vintage pieces found at auctions and sales. You can browse a showroom full of new leather recliners, reclaimed wood tables, and modern accessories, or roam through the large warehouse full of unfinished pieces waiting for someone to love them. You can even bring in your own heirloom piece to be custom painted.

3600 S 6th St., 217-503-6513

Here are a few other spots for fun furniture:

Tossed and Found
Corner of Lincoln and Madison streets, 217-793-9935

Flea Market to Fabulous
816 S. Spring St., 217-544-2322, www.fleamarket2fab.com

The Vintage Pinney
128 W. Editor St., Ashland, 217-415-5534

BID FOR BARGAINS
AT PATRICIA DOYLE AUCTION GALLERY

Need new bedroom furniture? Coveting some antique china? Can't live without a life-sized mannequin lamp? You never know what's going to be up for grabs at this weekly auction, but what better way to spend a Friday night? The gallery has a reputation for quality antiques and collectibles, but there are always deals to be had and plenty of hidden treasures in boxes that can sell for a few bucks.

3030 W. Jefferson St., 217-546-8709,
www.doyleauctions.com

HUNT FOR RUSTY TREASURES
AT THE LITCHFIELD PICKERS MARKET

Like junk? Then head to Litchfield, where this new market has grown into a great source for the rusty, the old, and the pre-loved. Vendors fill more than six city blocks with antiques, collectibles, and repurposed items on the second Sunday of each month from April through October. Local musicians play in the town's shaded park, which gives shoppers a place to rest on benches made from straw bales. Sometimes guests like Robbie Wolfe from the TV show *American Pickers* show up.

400 N. State St., Litchfield, 866-733-5833,
www.visitlitchfield.com

GET YOUR VINTAGE VINYL
AT RECYCLED RECORDS

Walk up the creaky steps to the second floor of this former furniture store, and you're likely to emerge several hours later with a stack of vintage vinyl and a big smile. Or dig into their inventory of cassettes, DVDs, CDs, stereo equipment, and vintage Playboys. It's all here. And if it isn't, the owners are happy to use their years of collecting experience to help you track it down.

625 E. Adams St., 217-522-5122,
www.recycledrecords.com

SHOP FOR CHARITY
AT DISTRICT 23

A mix of painted cottage furniture, jewelry, upcycled clothing, and wall art fill this charming brick house. Not only can you buy cool stuff, but you're donating to charity because the shop is run by volunteers of the Cochlear Implant Awareness Foundation, and all profits go to the cause. Limited hours include 4:30–6:30 p.m. Tuesdays and 10 a.m.–3 p.m. the first and third Friday and Saturday of each month.

1413 S. MacArthur Boulevard, 217-679-4643,
www.district23.com

SPEND AN AFTERNOON
IN ELKHART

Just 20 miles north of Springfield is small town charm at its best. It's easy to spend a few hours breathing in a blend of history, homemade pie, and quality antiques in a spot once occupied by Indian tribes. At the picturesque Elkhart Cemetery, visit the tomb of the three-term Illinois governor and Civil War general Richard J. Oglesby, among other eerily beautiful old gravesite markers. Shops on the downtown stretch include Birdsong Antiques, a shop filled with artfully arranged vintage clothing, art, and baubles. Stop at the Wild Hare Café for lunch and lively conversation with the friendly owners.

Route 66, between Springfield and Lincoln. 217-947-2046,
www.elkhartillinois.us

MAKE JEWELRY
AT LA BEAD, OH!

This small brick building filled to the brim with all things necessary to make jewelry is the opposite of a big box store. This is where you come for supplies and get a big dose of assistance, personal attention and inspiration on the side. Every corner is crammed with beads and materials to create your own jewelry—glass, clay, stone, metal, shell, wood, pearl, and African trade beads, as well as gemstones, crystals and metal chain, wire and thread. A large glass jar is filled with vintage Italian seed beads and one wall is dedicated to tubes of tiny beads in a rainbow of colors. The shop features two classrooms and a lobby area where students can learn a new technique, like bead stitching, enameling, and wire or metal work, taught by special guests from across the country, or local staff and jewelry experts. Special events and classes are held throughout the year, including a monthly summer class called Bead and Bauble, a class open to the public where for less than $8 you make a piece of jewelry to take home. You can even bring in your own project to work on in the lobby, where the staff will be glad to assist you. If you need a break, the shop shares space with an antique store where you can do some more shopping of a different kind.

1500 S. Sixth St., 217-544-8473,
www.labeadoh.com

TREAT YOURSELF
AT THE OLD CAPITOL ART FAIR

The Old State Capitol serves as a backdrop to this annual downtown event, when 150 juried artists fill the streets with art, from photography and ceramics to jewelry and sculpture. A children's tent invites children from pre-school through high school age to buy original art at special prices. For the adults, a wine tasting area is a great place to unwind.

Between Fifth and Sixth streets, 217-523-2787,
www.socaf.org

TIP

Tip: After a day of shopping, stop by Driftwood Eatery for a true taste of farm fresh fare, with a grazing menu of small plates like pickled veggies and chicken and waffles meant to be shared. The best cocktail list in town offers unique twists on classics like the Pink Gimlet and embraces the farmer's market motto with creative, herb-infused libations.

Corner 5th and Adams streets, 217-572-1906,
www.driftwoodeatery.com

Other local art fairs worth perusing:

Art Spectacular at the Carillon
Juried fine art and craft fair in an intimate park setting
with 50 artists, a silent auction, and music.

1740 W. Fayette Ave. and Chatham Rd.,
217-546-3853,
www.carillon-rees.org

Edwards Place Fine Art Fair
Artisans fill the shaded grounds around historic
Edwards Place, with live music, a used
book sale, and kids activities.

700 N. Fourth St., 217-523-2631,
www.springfieldart.org

FIND THE PERFECT GIFT
AT SIMPLY FAIR

This is the perfect place to find a gift for someone who has everything. Because they're probably not going to have all these handcrafted and fair-trade items from 40 nations, like recycled cement-bag totes from Vietnam or felted birdhouses from Nepal. Don't forget to sample the free chocolate and coffee.

2357 W. Monroe, 217-679-0591,
www.simplyfairtrade.com

SHOP FOR HOME DÉCOR
IN THE COUNTRY

What could be better than hunting for new treasures in a big old country shed? Hunting in two sheds! Salvage Unique Home Décor and Consignments is the place. A big barn holds vintage furniture and home accessories, found by the owners on frequent buying trips to Amish auctions in Indiana. The smaller shed, formerly a corn crib rebuilt from materials found on the eight-acre farm, is filled with shabby chic home decor. Crusty, farm-rough items like shutters, ladders, signs, and architectural salvage pieces are scattered outside. Kids will love the miniature petting zoo, with a pygmy goat and twin cows, plus 50 pet chickens eager to greet visitors. And did we mention the pygmy goat? Open seasonally May through October.

3803 N. Pleasant Plains Road,
County Highway 9C, Pleasant Plains, 217-685-6639

DIG THROUGH RARE BOOKS
AT PRAIRIE ARCHIVES

For some people, nothing beats scanning the shelves of a used book store in search of hidden treasures. The genius of Prairie Archives is that it offers treasures for all kinds of book lovers. You might stumble onto a rare treatise on history, a paperback sci-fi classic, or a coffee table book about your favorite painter. The shop even thinks about folks who just wander by after business hours—there are tables of books outside 24 hours a day. If you find one you want, just slip a dollar through the mail slot.

522 E. Adams St., 217-522-9742,
www.prairiearchives.com

BE A SHARP DRESSED MAN
AT JIM HERRON LTD.

With over 40 years of experience there's only one place to go for a custom-made suit, trousers, and even jeans! This is individual attention personified, with in-house tailoring and free alterations for the garment's lifetime. Located in a downtown hotel since 1985, this stylish and classic store is a reminder of how clothing stores used to be. Rows of trousers are hung properly on pant hangers, not stacked in piles atop tables, and dress shirts are neatly folded behind glass cases. Italian loafer socks, neckties, sports shirts, handmade silk ties, leather shoes, and tuxedos are also available—everything you need to be a sharp dressed man.

700 E. Adams St., 217-753-8036,
www.jimherronltd.com

Photo credit: Abraham Lincoln
Presidential Library and Museum

SUGGESTED
ITINERARIES

FOR THE FOODIES

Crunch on a Corn Dog at the Illinois State Fair, 2

Peruse Produce at the Farmers Market, 4

Try the Heat at Magic Kitchen, 12

Pig Out on Pot Pie at Café Moxo, 5

Blow Your Diet for Chocolate at Cocoa Blue, 24

Have Brunch in the Beer Garden at Boone's Saloon, 6

Feast on Fried Chicken at the Track Shack, 8

Eat a Plate-Sized Pancake at Charlie Parker's, 25

Pick Blueberries at Jefferies Orchard, 9

Indulge in Macarons at Incredibly Delicious, 10

Savor Soup at the Feed Store, 11

Dig in to a Horseshoe at D'Arcy's, 17

Celebrate Farm Fresh at American Harvest Eatery, 3

Savor Chilli at the Dew Chilli Parlor, 20

Sample Seasonal Morel Pie at Maldaner's, 21

Drive-Through the Maid-Rite, 28

WINE AND DINE

Listen to Local Jazz at Robbie's, 50

Take a Tour of Rolling Meadows Brewery, 14

Taste Wine at Danenberger Family Vineyards, 18

Enjoy Libations with a View in the Pinnacle Club Lounge, 29

Have Brunch in the Beer Garden at Boone's Saloon, 6

FREE FOR ALL

IT'S A DATE

ALL ABOUT ABE

FAMILY FUN

ONLY IN SPRINGFIELD

SHOP TILL YOU DROP

AL FRESCO ACTIVITIES

Photo credit: Penny Zimmerman-Wills

ACTIVITIES
BY SEASON

WINTER

Take a Spin on the Ice at the Nelson Center, 65

Enjoy the Holidays at the Dana-Thomas House, 82

Go Sledding at Centennial Park, 70

Watch the Junior Blues Take the Ice, 58

SPRING

Go Birdwatching at Adams Wildlife Sanctuary, 56

Enjoy Pork and Pottery for Art at SAA, 84

Drive the Mother Road, 88

Savor the Serenity of Lincoln Memorial Gardens, 64

Photo credit: Christopher Wills

INDEX

Photo credit: Penny Zimmerman-Wills